IN SEARCH OF A SOUL

RAYMOND MORIYAMA

IN SEARCH

DESIGNING AND REALIZING THE NEW CANADIAN WAR MUSEUM

OF A SOUL

DOUGLAS & McINTYRE

VANCOUVER/TORONTO

Douglas & McIntyre Ltd.
2323 Quebec Street, Suite 201
Vancouver, British Columbia
Canada V5T 4S7
www.douglas-mcintyre.com

Acknowledgement
Interested readers will also enjoy the documentary film:
"In Search of A Soul: Building the Canadian War Museum"
"À la mémoire du passé: Le Musée canadien de la guerre"
Produced by Sound Venture Productions
Writer/Director/Producer: Katherine Jeans
Executive Producer/Producer: Neil Bregman
DVDs available at www.soundventure.com
© 2005 Sound Venture Productions Ottawa Limited

Library and Archives Canada Cataloguing in Publication
Moriyama, Raymond
In search of a soul : designing and realizing the new
Canadian War Museum / Raymond Moriyama.

ISBN-13: 978-1-55365-207-6 · ISBN-10: 1-55365-207-X

1. Canadian War Museum. 2. Moriyama, Raymond.
3. Military museums—National Capital Region
(Canada)—Design and construction. 4. Museum architecture—
National Capital Region (Canada). I. Title.

NA6700.O88M67 2006   727'.635500971   C2006-901737-9

Editing by Scott Steedman
Jacket and text design by Peter Cocking
Jacket photographs © Brian Rudy, MTA (front)
and Tom Arban (back)
Printed and bound in by Canada by Friesens
Printed on acid-free paper
Distributed in the U.S. by Publishers Group West

We gratefully acknowledge the financial support of the Canada Council for the Arts, the British Columbia Arts Council, and the Government of Canada through the Book Publishing Industry Development Program (BPIDP) for our publishing activities.

CONTENTS

TO OUR TEN GRANDCHILDREN

INTRODUCTION

Exciting, challenging, arduous, spiritual, rewarding.

These words only begin to describe how I feel about designing and realizing the new Canadian War Museum. I struggled between happiness and frustration. In the process, memories of my first foray into architecture, long ago at the age of twelve, emerged from the deep crevices of my mind. Seeking solace from the degradations of life in an internment camp, I designed and secretly built a tree house on the side of Little Mountain, an elongated hill next to the Slocan River in the shadow of the Rockies. Remarkably, this spot shares many similarities with the war museum site in Ottawa. However, my tree house was not a museum—it became my sanctuary during wartime.

What led me to build a tree house? After Japan attacked Pearl Harbor in December 1941, all twenty-two thousand people of Japanese ancestry living in the coastal areas of British Columbia—mostly born in Canada—were rounded up as enemy aliens and shipped inland to various camps. My father refused to be separated from my pregnant mother, my two younger sisters and myself, so he was arrested and sent to a POW camp in Ontario; my mother then had a miscarriage and I lost the only brother I ever could have had.

Our internment camp had no private baths, just two public baths for men and women. I had large, visible scars caused by a boiling stew and aggravated by an incompetent doctor. Boys and even some adults taunted me in the bathhouse: "He's diseased, don't touch him!" "Ugly, ugly, ugly!" Humiliated by my own community and rejected by my country, I decided to escape and bathe in the Slocan River. I built a lookout nearby on the sloping bank. When I saw no one, I jumped in. The water was brutally cold, but it was better than hot tears. Nature, I soon realized, was beautiful and comforting, and did not make fun of my scars. Without a father to lean on, nature became my solace. My heart awakened, I began to transform the lookout into more than an aid for bathing.

1

Completing that tree house was a great challenge. I had no money and no help and did not dare to ask for any, as I was afraid that I would be discovered doing something illegal and sent to a POW camp far away. Who then would look after my mother and sisters? Building material was limited: natural green boughs, branches and scraps collected from a local sawmill; equipment, primitive: just a borrowed saw, a handful of nails and an axe. Maximizing the result was to be my initiation into architectural economy, a life lesson never to be forgotten.

Despite these limitations, the finished tree house was far beyond my expectations. Its rhombic form fused with the tree and blended so well into the natural surroundings that it was virtually invisible—ideal for eluding detection by security officers. Aesthetically, I thought it wonderful!

More importantly, that modest tree house offered a surprising new experience. It became a place of revelation. It exposed me to the many faces of nature and her immaculate balance: the sound of the wind at night, howling storms, the whispers of the river, serene moonlight in the mountains, crimson sunsets, the sweet fragrance of an autumn breeze, heavy and soft rain, sleet and icy snow. How wonderfully the animals and insects sheltered themselves and lived together. I even learned to wiggle my ears and twitch my nose studying them.

And, to my amazement, every square foot of land below me was different from the next square foot, and the next one and the next. Is the whole world like this, I wondered, every square foot unique unto itself? It was magic. I became Christopher Columbus in this undiscovered world. That tree house was my private school in the trees, a place of happy unstructured learning. It introduced me to solace, to solitude, to contemplation and to many inexplicable facets of life and human nature. In my sanctuary, I developed a new understanding of myself, of nature, of Canada and of the fragility of democracy.

Rhomboid
Tree House
1942-43
Slocan-Bay farms, B.C.   LM

It seems ironic yet appropriate that, nearly six decades later, I, a Vancouver-born Canadian and a former inmate of a Canadian internment camp, would be commissioned to lead an architectural joint venture to design the new Canadian War Museum, not as a monument or a mausoleum, but as a living repository of the experiences and memories of wars and peace-keeping involving Canadians.

Since the official opening of the new museum on May 8, 2005, many people have asked me to tell my story. Many more have raised questions about the project that have not yet been answered. And others are unwittingly circulating misinformation about my life and about the ideas and thinking that shaped the new museum. So, before memory fades, I have decided to write about my experience, to record my thoughts and feelings and explain my search to embody the soul of a nation. I write not only to preserve a record of my experiences, but also to thank and pay homage to the many individuals who contributed greatly to this important institution and who enriched my journey in countless ways. As I wrestle with my journalistic mandate, one thing has become absolutely clear: I am a better architect than a raconteur or writer.

THE COMMISSION It took decades of lobbying by veterans and the blood, sweat and tears of many tenacious supporters before the decision was made to create a new Canadian War Museum. The old museum, a stone fortresslike structure on Sussex Drive in downtown Ottawa, was too small and environmentally inappropriate for displaying and properly expressing Canadian military history. After much wrangling, including many battles between veterans and the government, a brave decision was reached during a period of cutbacks to treat "Canada's war history properly." First, in the late 1990s, the government announced that a site had been found in a rather inconvenient location next to the aviation museum in Ottawa's east end. Then, in May 2001, Sheila Copps, then minister of Heritage, announced that a new piece of land had been found in a more central spot west of the Parliamentary Precinct in LeBreton Flats.

In the summer of 2001, an invitation was issued to architects internationally to submit a response to a request for information (RFI) presenting their qualifications. My firm, Moriyama & Teshima Architects (MTA) of Toronto, submitted a joint-venture proposal with Griffiths Rankin

5

Cook (GRC) of Ottawa. We were shortlisted and invited to submit a request for proposal (RFP) including the details of all key team members, our design philosophy, how the project was to be carried out, a rough schedule and a fee proposal. With the other finalists—I believe there were four or five—we were then invited to Ottawa in October 2001.

The Architect Selection Committee interviewed us on October 16 in the boardroom of the Museum of Civilization. Alex Rankin, John Cook, Don Cruikshank, my son Jason Moriyama and I represented our proposal. I had faith in the design team we had assembled and wanted us to receive the commission based on our collective talent, experience, imagination, dedication and organizational ability. We were informed that we had won the commission shortly after the interview. We were absolutely ecstatic; I also felt a weighty responsibility. This was to be an exciting challenge, a blood-stirring adventure.

The schedule was tight but doable: a research and design start date of November 2001; a substantial architectural completion by the end of November 2004; and, as the saying goes, a race against the clock to open on May 8, 2005, the sixtieth anniversary of VE Day.

A few members of the Architect Selection Committee later told me that they believed I combined a passion for architecture with a unique understanding of museums and unstructured learning. They were convinced that, with myself as principal design architect, the joint-venture team would create a uniquely Canadian solution that would exceed the institutional mandate to "Remember, Preserve and Educate / Commémorer, Préserver et Éduquer."

None of the museum's board members or senior members of the administration ever mentioned or asked about my wartime experiences. I never raised the subject either—not until the summer of 2004, when I was invited to be a part of an exhibit on the Japanese-Canadian "relocation" during World War II. I declined. It was enough to be involved as an architect; to be exposed in an exhibit would have been too much.

At the interview with the Architect Selection Committee, I made a personal commitment, not only to fulfill a special Canadian need and to do our best to open on time, but also to devote myself completely to the project until the end of design development, scheduled for early 2003. I was intending to retire from my architectural practice soon after that date, but this was not to be.

PERSONAL REVELATIONS

During the design and construction of the museum, I recognized within myself the same excitement I had felt as a youth building that tree house. Construction workers who shared a similar passion for their work reinforced this feeling. On one occasion, I was greeted on the site with a heartwarming masculine hug from a seasoned concrete worker who enthused, "I am excited by the challenges I face every day, every hour." Another veteran worker proudly announced, "I'm bringing my grandkids here to show them what grandpa did to build this war museum!" I had been asking them, in good humour yet in all seriousness, to aspire to build a perfect museum with "imperfect," dilapidated walls peppered with bullet holes, such as would be found in a war zone. I was asking them to unlock their minds and open the doors of their creative ability—to become partners in realizing something special.

Tony Bellai of Bellai Brothers and his team of near seniors completed the concrete work to perfection. They are mentioned here as representatives of all of the committed and skilled workers and suppliers on the job. For a contemporary architect, encountering this kind of on-site enthusiasm and pride is rare. I felt elated by our relationship, propelled by the poem my father had given me, beautifully hand scripted, at my high-school graduation:

> Into God's temple of eternity,
> Drive a nail of gold.

My father did not ask me to build the temple or even to consider designing it. A gentle teacher, he was simply asking me to drive a single nail into God's temple of eternity, just one, but one forged of gold. A little while later on the site of the war museum, I couldn't help thinking, *Do the enthusiastic passions of these builders signify golden things to come?* Quietly, I was hoping so, and I wondered whether one of my callings was to help open more doors of hidden and potentially golden creativity. I felt oddly constrained by the limits of my own knowledge and by the untapped potential of others—things we do not realize we are capable of, or that we keep hidden under the guise of conventional wisdom.

On another occasion, while walking over a field of reinforcing bars on the roof, I was struck by a naive yet genuine thought—perhaps I was put on earth and granted the miracle of life for the purpose of bringing architectural birth to this new museum. In my heart, this thought did not feel like an exaggeration. At the age of four I suffered life-threatening burns and it was during my recovery, when I was bedridden and trying to distract myself from the pain by focusing intently upon a construction project across the street, that I decided to become an architect. They say that God opens a door for every child, and for me, the moment was born in pain.

Later, at the age of nine, another door was opened for me. This time I was riding a transit train with my father from Vancouver to New Westminster and watching the city go by—all the different people and street activities, the huge variety of stores, the Carnegie Library on the corner of Hastings and Main and Chinatown next door, the railway terminal on Main Street, so many cars and trucks, then open space and parkland. In the distance, mountains emerged and disappeared behind buildings. Someone must design cities too, I thought. And I decided then and there that after becoming an architect, I would also become an urban planner and designer. It seemed a reasonable plan.

But one cannot always control the course of one's plans, and only a few years later I found myself in an internment camp, a prisoner within my own country. These decidedly profound events were my foundation. In the sixty years that followed, I dedicated myself to learning about life, about Canada and Canadians, about cultural and social diversity and inclusion, and about architecture and urban design. If somehow fate had brought me to this project—and in my heart, I believed this was true—then I decided that I had to remain personally invested in it and continue overseeing the design, to ensure that the original philosophy, vision, timing and budget were realized.

Was it my ambition, I have been asked, to change the direction of Canadian architecture with this project, to alter criteria and approaches to the whole design process? Yes and no; all such stories are exaggerated fictions. I had concluded very early on that the project was all about finding one special solution for this one specific national project—a solution that, ideally, would provide a unique personal experience for every single visitor, Canadian and international. This building was not to be just about architecture or about fulfilling the personal vision of one architect; it was to be about responding to the diverse perspectives of individual visitors, about expressing the contradictions and ambiguities of war and sacrifice. Most importantly, I wanted the building to compel resolve, big or small, within each visitor, to make them think hard about themselves, the nation and the world. I wasn't expecting to find any answers, but I wanted to raise questions in the visitor's mind. And I wanted to carry out the project on time and more

economically than the construction of any other national museum, while responding to the natural and urban context and to issues of sustainability.

This, then, is the story of my experience—my search for a soul and an architecture of meaning—my thoughts and dilemmas, fears and expectations, sadness and elation at designing and realizing the new Canadian War Museum in our nation's capital.

THE TEAM

The search for meaning may be an individual act, but it should be understood that architecture, like a symphony, is not the product of one architect alone. The new Canadian War Museum (CWM) is no exception. It owes its existence to literally thousands of talented and devoted individuals working hard as a team. I am sure every one of them can recall wonderful stories—funny, sad and serious—and heroic efforts made, despite numerous impediments, to realize this special place.

We all did our best: architects, consultants, contractors, builders, suppliers and tradespeople; our client, the National Capital Commission (NCC), the City of Ottawa and the local authorities; museum staff and exhibit designers; renderers, model-makers and photographers. Nearly everyone involved in this remarkable project seemed to understand that they were a part of something special and that their personal best was required. I owe much to them all and, by this account, extend my personal appreciation and gratitude to the entire team, including all those wonderful people— veterans and interested members of the public alike—who shared with us their inspired thoughts and ideas.

THE INDIVIDUAL

Although architecture is the work of many, the founding concept and the quest for a soul and a philosophy in a particular design originate with one individual. This same individual, the principal design architect, also has the final word on the overall design and on all significant details.

If I had simply followed the client's requirements—which had been beautifully detailed and meticulously documented by Michael Lundholm, a professional programmer—the work of our design team would have been simpler, especially for myself. No dilemmas. No struggles. No sleepless nights. On the other hand, there would have been no innovation. No discovery. No fun. No stirring of blood. Our mandate transcended a mere checklist of requirements, and I found myself pondering issues impossible to include in such a list.

I was fortunate to have my son Jason working with me on the project. With his architecture degree and industrial-design background, he was a heavenly intellect and a patient and conscientious devil's advocate. He tenaciously worked out many of the difficult public spaces, made careful calculations, resolved many difficult details and helped me make clearer decisions. He deserves much of the credit for our most courageous results.

PASSIONATE DISINTERESTEDNESS

From the day I started a one-man practice in 1958, an architect in our office was never considered a knight in shining armour riding a white charger, nor the sun around which the universe revolved, nor a know-it-all professional with an answer for everything. In those days, such condescending and arrogant attitudes were prevalent, but I was raised to believe that "even a monkey can fall from a tree."

If we were asked directly, we preferred to say that an architect could be a moon. Just as the Moon reflects light from the Earth, the Sun, the stars and the universe, so too an architect receives the light of inspiration from other outside sources—and like the Moon, the architect absorbs and mixes what is received and reflects back a new and different kind of light, an enlightenment that is understated, suggestive, humane and deeply felt. Striving to be the Moon and not the Sun was striving to practise architecture with a quality I call "passionate disinterestedness."

As an attitude, passionate disinterestedness has always allowed us at MTA to be involved intimately and passionately with our work, but also to step away from ourselves and to view our thinking and its context more objectively, even to relax and laugh at ourselves. It is an approach that stops us from churning out homogeneous and dogmatic design solutions, which only lead to ubiquitous architecture. By contrast, passionate disinterestedness allows us to express sensuous ambiguity and specificity, human richness and cultural pluralism and social inclusion in our work.

MIND YOUR Ps AND Ls

THE FIVE Ps

Striving to be a moon, MTA used an analytical method known as the Five Ps developed by my partner, Ted Teshima. The Five Ps reference five areas of analysis that, undertaken at the outset of a project, ensure a wonderful, fresh process and result every time. The Five Ps are as follows:

1. *People*—client, users, general public, the nation
2. *Place*—natural and built, weather, geography, ecology, climate
3. *Program*—stated, unstated, past, future
4. *Process*—timing, costing, construction, approvals
5. *Philosophy*—values, ideology, spirituality, customs, mores

The first four Ps often lead to objective, intellectually satisfying answers, but taken together with the fifth P, Philosophy, the Five Ps raise issues and questions that are often hidden, subtle and ignored. Analyzing all five engenders approaches and solutions that are always humane, sensuously intellectual, natural and often courageous.

THE THREE Ls

Another process that guides the work of MTA is one we like to call the Three Ls. We practise the Three Ls on every project to broaden our understanding of client, user and passive citizen needs, and to address conflicts and important ideas. The Three Ls are as follows:

1. *Listen.* Listen carefully to others. It is said that if you listen well enough, you will have no questions to ask.
2. *Learn.* Strive to learn from others by listening well and by additional research.
3. *Leadership.* Lead with wisdom and an open heart, and work to earn leadership and respect in design.

I came to realize the importance of listening in the tree house. I used to think, if the government had only listened to the voices of my Japanese-Canadian community, I would have had my father with us rather than far away in a POW camp, my mother would not have had a miscarriage and I would have had the younger brother I wanted so much, and I would not have been so lonely, suspended upside-down with no firm foundation. Instead of listening and learning, the government jumped to deeds on the basis of distorted preconceptions and prejudice, not facts or reality.

I vowed then to listen and learn before I responded or took action. I thought a great deal about human insensitivity and the loss of spiritual growth, especially in children caught in war. I came to realize that I would have a lot to do when I became an architect and a planner, and told myself that one of my most important considerations would be the inclusion of all people, young and old, healthy and handicapped (one of my closest friends had a club foot).

The thoughtful application of the Ps and Ls to our work has served us well over the years, and remains a strong component of our culture at MTA. In November of 2001, the Three Ls were instrumental in getting the war museum project onto the right track from the outset.

THE PROCESS

LISTENING TO CANADIANS Pre-design research for the war museum commenced in mid-November 2001. While our inspiration for the design was drawn from many sources, the heart of our inspiration came from listening carefully to Canadians articulating their thoughts on war and war museums.

For this critical input and inspiration, I travelled across Canada with Joe Geurts, the director and CEO of the CWM, to listen to Canadians and to learn, distill and apply their ideas. The itinerary included stops on the east coast and in Montreal, Ottawa, Toronto and Calgary. As one can imagine, the range of thoughts and opinions about war and a war museum was vast, yet one thing became evident: there was a clear divergence of view between the sexes.

Women tended to speak of home fronts and of universal suffering, expressed in phrases such as "going to the depths of hell to resurrect the soul," and not in terms of who was right or who was wrong. Men, by contrast, spoke of heroics, of good times and bad, and of the direct experiences of war and peacekeeping. Many asked that war not be glorified. A few veterans were adamant about the economics and capital costs of the project, advising "Don't spend too much money but make it great!"

The perspectives and ideas we heard were influenced also by the multicultural character of Canada. Our citizens now come from over two hundred countries and speak more than a hundred and forty languages and dialects, reflecting a multitude of different religions, cultures and social habits. Clearer understanding of diversity and inclusion was necessary. Many new Canadians, especially the youth, had little understanding of the sacrifices and experiences of our veterans and only a slim knowledge not only of Canada's military history, but also of Canadian history in general. As one veteran chuckled, "We can't laugh at the Americans, who at least know their own history."

Finally, many Canadians reminded us that the museum needed to be entertaining, interactive and fun to visit if it was to attract and sustain interest. I realized that the new museum would have to appeal to all of these audiences and somehow reflect all of the input we had received. Clearly, imagination, innovation and a guiding philosophy were essential; we would have to go beyond architecture.

IN SEARCH OF MEANING

"An impeccable architect gives up a part of his ego to embody the soul of the nation he serves." These were the words of advice I was given by a wise lady in the early days of the project. "If this is so," I asked her, "then what is to be the 'soul' of the new Canadian War Museum?" "That's for you to find out," she answered with a divine smile.

So many questions swirled in my head. In designing a new war museum, do we dare think only of wars, death, sacrifices and heroics, without thinking philosophically of the future and of the hopes of mankind yet unfulfilled? How can an architecture reflecting the ambience of war add to the visitor's experience without overpowering the exhibits or glorifying war? Can we use non-programmed areas such as corridors and back stairs as museum "experience" spaces? Can architecture itself be an exhibit? Can we enhance and strengthen the institution's international reputation and its mandate to "Remember, Preserve and Educate" by being more distinctly Canadian? Could images of nature—trees and landscapes—in war zones shape the philosophy and the forms of the design? What

is the Ottawa site, both the natural and built environments, telling us? What can we bring to the thinking to help the design stand the test of time? What would we answer if soldiers killed in centuries past came back and asked, "What have you learned from our sacrifice?" How can we balance and achieve economy, good design and sustainability? What is Canadian? What does war mean? What is the soul of a Canadian war museum?

SOURCES OF INSPIRATION

DEEDS OF CANADIAN PEOPLE

Our team of architects and designers first looked to the peoples of Canada for inspiration. In addition to the input received while travelling across the country, I also talked to Canadians in subways, buses, trains, planes, restaurants, libraries and universities in Toronto, Vancouver, St. Catharines, Niagara Falls and Ottawa. In fact, I was interested in the view of virtually every person I encountered during that time. Many talked about wars in distant lands, and even "wars" within Canada.

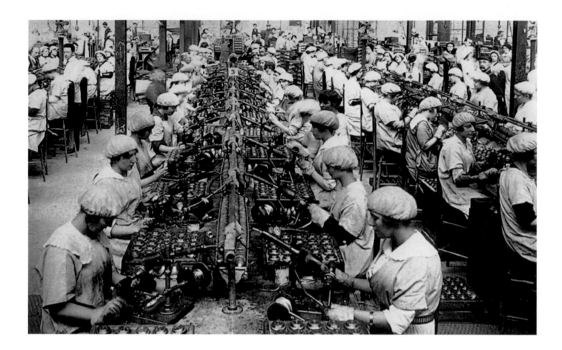

I also heard the voices of Canada's First Nations people in Ottawa, where I was invited by the Honourable Ethel Blondin-Andrew to meet a large number of representatives from across Canada. Many of them were very interested in the museum, though many also feared their stories would be ignored. I assured them that would not be the case. Some were cynical, and for a few, the idea of inclusion was a distant fantasy. Some may have considered me an Uncle Tom.

The Japanese-Canadian community thought that its experience of wartime discrimination and internment would be treated lightly, as a minor incident and not as an important story, a black mark in the history of Canadian "democracy" for future generations to learn from. Chinese Canadians expressed similar thoughts about the Chinese head tax. Some community members questioned the Canadian government's attitudes towards Ukrainians in the early days and to Jewish immigrants during World War II. Old scabs were scratched, emotional wounds exposed. Many of the stories were not pleasant to hear, yet all the speakers shared a wish for a brighter future of inclusion and hope. And I was very encouraged by the comments in Montreal, where French Canadians expressed the need for a national war museum to acknowledge the contributions made by Québécois and other Canadians.

All this input served to point us in a spiritual direction that felt Canadian. We pored over images and stories of war involving Canadians. We read about the unfathomable loss of life at the Battle of Vimy Ridge, where Canadian troops experienced one of their first major victories during World War I. The images of another World War I battlefield, Beaumont Hamel, moved me deeply and haunt me still. There, I learned, over seven hundred Newfoundlanders were killed or maimed fighting in trenches only a hundred yards apart. The hundreds of bomb craters, six to eight feet deep and now carpeted by green vegetation, must have run red with blood at the end of the battle.

Over and over we gazed upon photographs of heroic soldiers fighting in wasted landscapes and keeping peace on foreign lands, and we were ceaselessly amazed by the unselfish deeds of Canadians in extraordinary situations at home and in battle. And so emerged one of our greatest inspirations, which, to paraphrase Jack L. Granatstein, one of Canada's outstanding historians, can be summarized thus: *"Ordinary Canadians doing extraordinary deeds in exceptional times and circumstances."*

LANDSCAPES SCARRED BY WAR

Another source of inspiration were images of battles, wartorn towns and war-ravaged landscapes.

Siegfried Sassoon, a young British soldier who fought in World War I and became known as the "accidental hero" through his poetry about the horrors of war, memorialized one notable series of evocative images in his 1918 poem "Memorial Tablet":

> *. . . I died in hell—*
> *(They called it Passchendaele). My wound was slight,*
> *And I was hobbling back; and then a shell*
> *Burst slick upon the duck-boards: so I fell*
> *Into the bottomless mud, and lost the light.*

In only four months in 1917, the entire Belgian town of Passchendaele was reduced to a field of mud in which thousands of soldiers lost their lives. Only branchless trees remained after the onslaught, looking like lost, limbless souls.

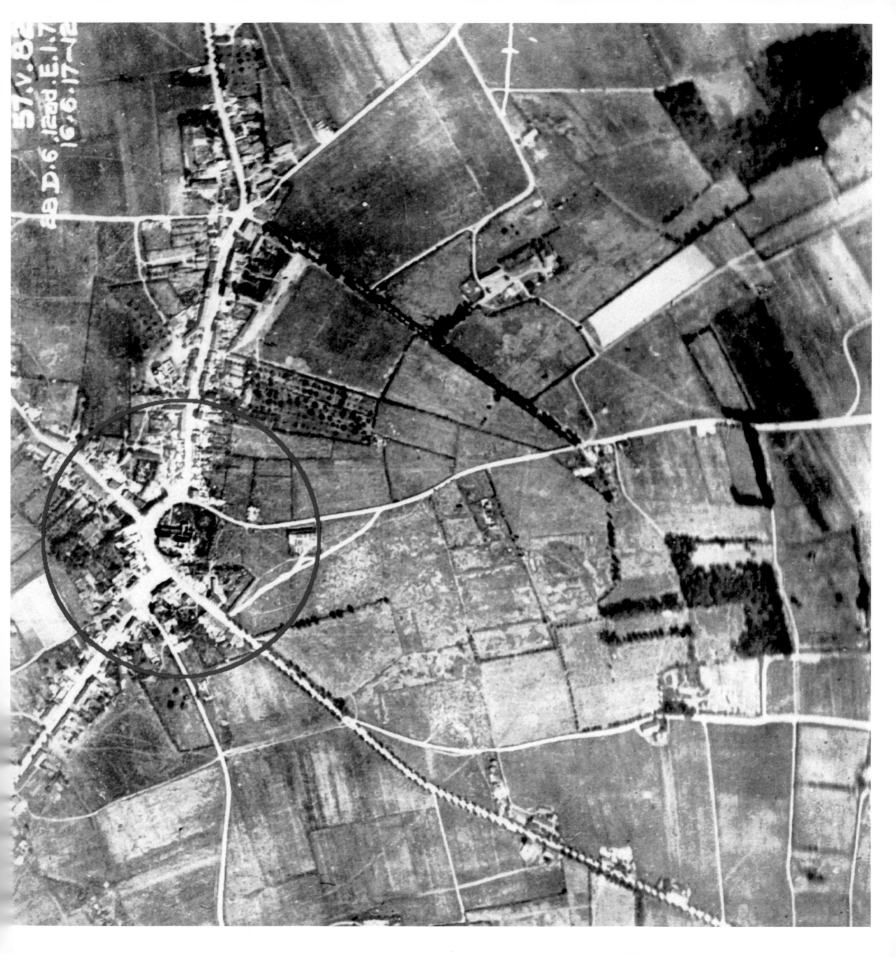

CANADIAN LANDSCAPES

Another source of inspiration was the diverse geological forms and landscapes found across Canada: the rocky Atlantic shorelines, the colours of nature in the eastern provinces, the glacier-worn rock formations around the Great Lakes, the vast grasslands and foothills of the Prairies, the snow-covered expanses of the Far North and the rugged magnificence of the Rockies and the mountains of the Pacific coast. It is my hope that the public will recognize these forms and themes reflected in the design.

THE COLLECTION

The CWM collection is extraordinarily impressive. I was deeply moved when I first viewed it, especially the artworks, and would challenge any nation to show us better art related to war. Name any famous Canadian artist and his or her work is there in the collection. Imagine a collection with four hundred works by Alex Colville! Some have estimated the value of the museum's art collection alone at as much as $1 billion CAD. The collection of military artifacts and memorabilia is equally impressive, and includes valuable medals, delicate written documents, original letters, hand-drawn maps and hundreds of uniforms (some with bloodstains, like the one General Brock was wearing when he was shot and killed during the War of 1812).

This vitally important content requires safe storage, strict environmental controls and protection from vandalism and flooding. At the same time, the museum that houses it must be able to display this content in an accessible, appropriate, enjoyable and educational manner. The heavy artifacts—artillery, vehicles, airplanes and a fifty-four-tonne Centurion tank—require not only a substantial volume of space, but also special floor loading and ceiling supports. The design of appropriate displays that respected the unique and precious qualities of every artifact, from paintings and medals to love letters and uniforms, was one of our most challenging tasks.

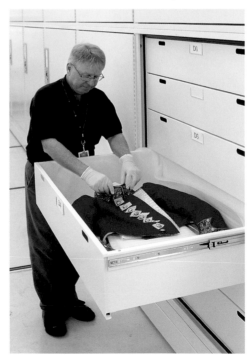

CWM SITE

The project site is a 7.5-hectare (18.5-acre) parcel on Ottawa's LeBreton Flats, an early industrial area on the banks of the Ottawa River. Facing east towards the Parliamentary Precinct, it is urban and profoundly nationalistic. The Peace Tower, Canada's national landmark, soars three hundred feet into the air, a strong symbol of the country's democracy and decision-making in times of peace and war. Other national landmarks display the traditional vernacular of Ottawa: steep roofs and towers clad in beautifully patinated copper.

The site has a second face to the west—one that is wonderfully pastoral. It overlooks an upstream reach of the river and enjoys spectacular sunsets. In summer, the sun sets over Quebec; in winter, over Ontario; during the spring and fall equinox, it sets straight over the Ottawa River. Is this symbolic? In summer, the breeze off the river is remarkably refreshing; in winter, the prevailing northwest wind is bitingly cold.

In spite of its profound beauty, the site also posed a number of real challenges, notably contaminated soil from early industrial uses and—given its proximity to the river—a very real potential for catastrophic flooding.

The site offered up another curse or—if viewed creatively—a potential gift. Probes indicated solid bedrock at a relatively shallow depth, sloping gently downwards towards the northwest. This bedrock allowed us to establish the limits of the contaminated soil, all of which had to be removed. It could also help to relieve the potentially cata-strophic flood risk. It was a further gift if the architectural design could take advantage of its natural contour, relating the bedrock to underground parking, structural supports, concrete walls and areas for storage and for displaying large and heavy artifacts, such as the Centurion tank.

Economically and ecologically, there was another risk to the site: Ottawa is in an earthquake zone, which could prove to be a curse if blasting provoked a tremor. However, on the balance sheet of pros and cons, nature was emerging as an exciting "pro."

MEANING OF THE 9-METRE DIMENSION

Photographs and paintings of men at the battlefront often show them marching in a single line. There is a significant reason for this. In our early research my partner, Diarmuid Nash, discovered that, in dire moments of battle, the balance between life and death rested within a 9-metre corridor: 4.5 metres to the right and 4.5 metres to the left. This corridor represented the zone within which a soldier could meet his enemy in hand-to-hand combat with a chance of surviving the encounter. Beyond lay no-man's land, a zone that no soldier could individually defend.[*]

From various pragmatic standpoints—architecturally, structurally and economically—this dimension works extremely well. It can be divided into 4.5- and 3-metre modules, works well for parking garage layout, is effective for architectural planning and layout, and offers economies in construction. Beyond this, I wondered whether, in the case of a war museum, it could provide a greater meaning, perhaps symbolic?

11 / 11 / 11: REMEMBRANCE DAY

Canadians have traditionally guarded a special place in their hearts for the observance of Remembrance Day. The period of silence and reverence at 11:00 a.m. is almost sacred to us: it is a moment at which we become quietly connected to one another and collectively connected to the past, a moment in which we confront the power of our vulnerability within the circle of life.

I have always believed that this date and time, the eleventh hour of the eleventh day of the eleventh month, should be immortalized in a physical way, and the war museum presented a perfect opportunity. Yet our mandate was silent on this point, so the question of what we as architects could do to achieve this immortalization within the museum loomed large. If we could find a way to immortalize this moment in time, would the endeavour somehow nurture the collective soul? Did the key to the design of such a monument rest within nature or within the Peace Tower, or within an integrated combination of both? More questions whirled through my mind...

* Graves, Donald, *Fighting for Canada: Seven Battles 1758–1945* (Toronto: R. Brass Studio, 2000).

In our search for meaning, grappling with questions, fears and uncertainties, we read and reread and read again the poetry of war: poems by Canadian soldiers and poems from other nations. One poem that evoked a powerful image was Carl Sandburg's "Grass":

Pile the bodies high at Austerlitz and Waterloo.
Shovel them under and let me work—
    I am the grass; I cover all.

And pile them high at Gettysburg
And pile them high at Ypres and Verdun.
Shovel them under and let me work.
Two years, ten years, and passengers ask the conductor:
    What place is this?
    Where are we now?

    I am the grass.
    Let me work.

These dramatic words mixed into the roiling sea of ideas, questions, memories and instinct from which I was hoping to draw inspiration. And still there were more questions...

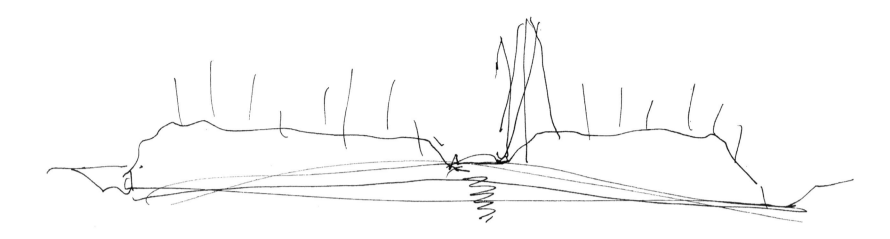

THE SOUND OF THE WIND

I had vividly experienced the sound of the wind one dark evening long ago in the sanctuary of my tree house. I remember it even now—eerie yet oddly comforting. In my mind
and in my solitude, I imagined the wind blowing over a silent battlefield, dark and
raw after a day of fierce fighting; and I imagined the soldiers from both sides in their
trenches, sheltering in tense exhaustion, their faces filled with fear and hope. I suppose
such images were not unusual for a youth such as I was, living in a state of unease and
periodic despair, facing unknowns and seeking comfort and solace in a wartime camp.
Even then my mind questioned: What is nature saying? What does the wind bring?

In the early stages of our work on the museum, the memory of that soft, ambiguous
wind returned to me and inspired my very first sketch: the Gatineau Hills across the
Ottawa River to the left, the sound of the wind in the tree house and Little Mountain
on the right. And still more questions: Was the wind a symbol of sacrifice? In the right
museum space, could the sound of the wind be more powerful and evocative than
music or words around a clutter of artifacts? Should there be a subtle tribute to our lost
heroes on top of the building, an extension above the roof, something that could hum
the song of the wind?

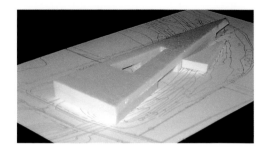

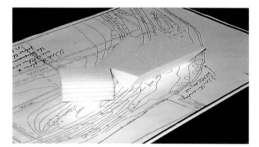

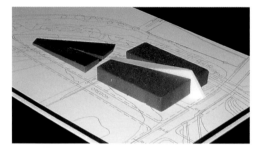

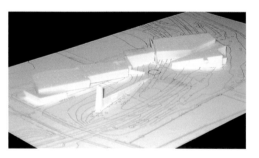

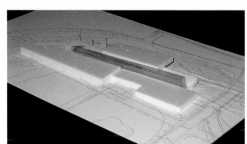

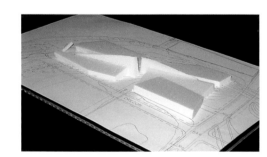

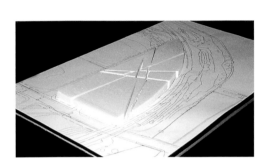

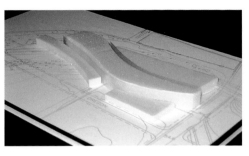

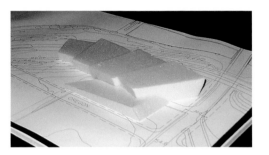

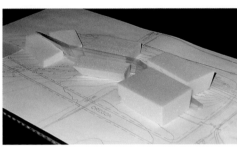

ONLY SIXTY-FOUR DESIGNS GENERATED

The process of architectural design is never a straight line. It is an exciting search and a struggle that I love. The war museum was a particularly intense personal struggle, the proof of which lies in the almost absurd fact that we generated not one, not two, not even five or ten, but sixty-four independent designs, each with a conceptual model and each assessed against a battery of criteria. Many of my friends, architects and non-architects alike, thought that this was foolish and self-indulgent; others expressed awe at our apparent willingness to risk the economic suicide of our architectural practice.

In defence of this seeming obsession, we felt compelled to explore every option in our search for a design that would stir the collective soul. If history judges our work as "indulgent," then I say in all sincerity that our indulgence, such as it was, was not for the self but was for the people of Canada—those who honour and those they come to honour.

THREE DETAILED DESIGNS FOR THE NATIONAL WEBSITE

The selection of themes and models was reduced from sixty-four to twenty-four and then to twelve. From these, the client selected three final designs.

The final designs were each developed and rendered in full by three in-house, yet separate and competing, design teams in Toronto. An independent quantity surveyor, Hanscomb Limited of Ottawa, estimated the capital costs and then, to fulfill the condition of our commission, the final three schemes were posted on the Canadian War Museum website.

The response to this "online charrette" was overwhelming—the museum received more than twelve hundred e-mails from an interested public in approximately two weeks. We were reassured by the fact that only 4 per cent of the Canadians who responded to the survey objected to building a new war museum.

NUMBER SIXTY-FIVE: THE FINAL DESIGN

We carefully reviewed the public input and took into account the war museum board's desire to have a vertical element. Then we produced a new hybrid design, the sixty-fifth. On June 23, 2002, in Edmonton, the board enthusiastically approved this final design, which was named "Regenerative Landscape" and included "Regeneration Hall," a new space incorporating a gently sloping vertical. The philosophy of "regeneration" and the broader view of war including "hope" were embraced by the board; these ideas are elaborated in the next section, "Design."

DESIGN

REGENERATION: A DESIGN PHILOSOPHY   As a result of our soul-searching, research and analysis, *regeneration* emerged as the word that best encapsulated the ideas and values at the heart of our philosophical approach.

The process of regeneration follows a sequence: *devastation, survival, rebirth, adaptation* and finally *life*. In times of war, nature is ravaged and seemingly destroyed. Miraculously and inevitably, however, nature survives and reclaims the devastation as the power of life prevails. It is this process of regeneration and healing that nourishes and rekindles human hope, faith and courage.

REGENERATIVE LANDSCAPES: THE ARCHITECTURAL CONCEPT Ours was to be an architecture of remembrance and regeneration. Our building would house the memories of devastation and sacrifice while expressing the power of survival and rebirth, acting as a visceral link between the "truths" of yesterday and the possibilities of tomorrow. And we wanted to create a unique yet economical design solution that functioned as a museum, complemented its physical and cultural surroundings, and expressed the strength and modesty of average Canadians.

Thus, the new Canadian War Museum emerges gently, almost invisibly, from the Ottawa River, growing gradually out of the grassy pastoral landscape of LeBreton Flats. As it rises towards the east and the urban cityscape, its grass-covered roof turns to copper to reflect Ottawa's urban vernacular, particularly the traditional copper-capped Parliamentary Precinct. There are no vertically thrusting towers, only subtle representations of geological forms from across Canada. The overall feeling is horizontal, more landscaping than building. In the end, the ordinary is rendered quietly nationalistic and extraordinary.

REGENERATION DEMANDS SUSTAINABILITY

The architectural concept of *Regenerative Landscape* demanded that our design and construction strategies embrace principles of sustainability and energy conservation without compromising the control over the internal environment required to protect valuable artifacts. Doing so despite budgetary constraints was a design priority. Reducing the load on municipal services was also an important consideration.

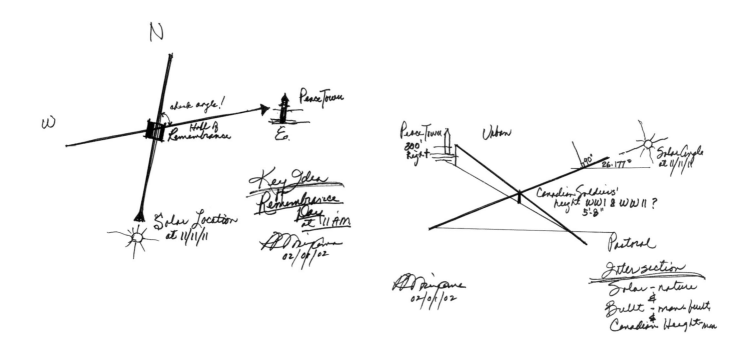

REGENERATION OF VISITORS

I did not design the architecture of the Canadian War Museum to be loved.

After the public input and all our research, I came to believe that "a beautiful conventional building" was the last thing a new war museum needed to be in the twenty-first century. My objective, stated bluntly and perhaps a little pompously, was to create a building that not only enhances the exhibits and the institution, but also moves visitors emotionally, that makes them feel something different and extraordinary. I want them to think, to question, to go through an emotional and physical process and arrive, hopefully, at rebirth. I want visitors to confront some dark truths and come away feeling rejuvenated, full of resolve, small or big, to face the future.

THE INTERSECTION OF NATURE AND THE MAN-MADE

A key part of the design was based on the intersection of nature and the man-made: the angle and location of the sun's rays at precisely 11:00 a.m. on Remembrance Day, November 11, and the view angle and location of the Peace Tower, Canada's symbol of democratic decision-making in peacetime and war. These intersections were sketched out in two drawings made very early in the design process.

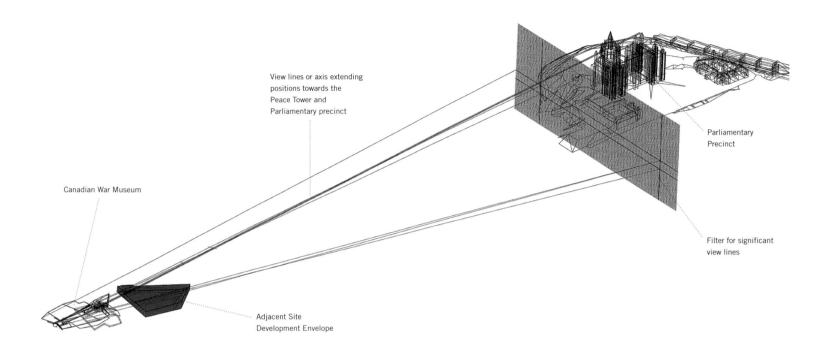

View lines or axis extending
positions towards the
Peace Tower and
Parliamentary precinct

Canadian War Museum

Parliamentary
Precinct

Filter for significant
view lines

Adjacent Site
Development Envelope

THE VIEW CORRIDOR TO AND FROM THE PEACE TOWER

I was personally heartened by the National Capital Commission's promise to preserve a
view corridor between the War Museum and the Peace Tower, to honour the symbolic
link between these two important buildings. And I will go a step further and say that,
in my view, if this visual link upon which the very orientation and design of the CWM is
based is somehow destroyed or, worse, forgotten, Ottawa and the NCC will have a dear
cost to pay to the veterans, the nation and future generations. The view corridor that
dictated the design is explained above in a diagram.

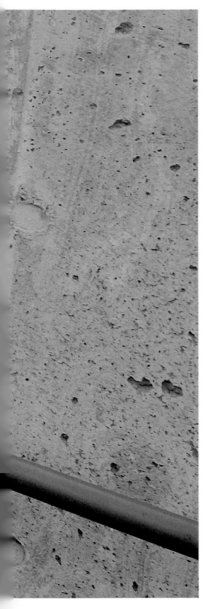

GREEN ROOF The green roof—an assembly of local, self-seeding plant materials—helps to insulate the building while integrating it with the natural landscape of the Ottawa riverside. Green roofs also reduce storm-water runoff. In urban settings, the volume of water that flows off roofs, roads and other impervious surfaces exceeds our storm-water management capacities; green roofs hold rain like sponges and allow nature to dissipate the moisture naturally. Vegetation protects the roof from extreme temperatures and lowers the temperature of the surrounding urban environment. It also reduces a building's energy requirements by keeping down the ambient temperature of the roof's surface, which mitigates the transfer of heat into the building.

Green roofs also reduce air and noise pollution and protect the roof structure itself from heat, ultraviolet radiation and physical abuse, making a roof longer lasting and more cost-effective and sustainable. Although the design and construction of such a large green roof system certainly had its challenges, the environmental benefits more than justified the undertaking.

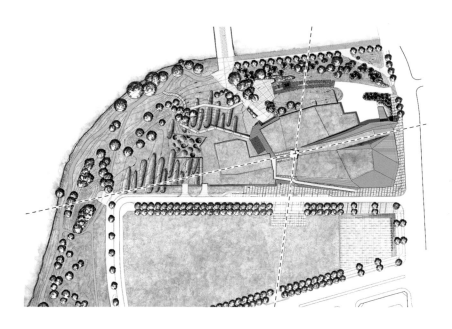

LANDSCAPING

The northern and western edges of the building are integrated with the Riverside Promenade and the river beyond by natural landscaping. The outdoor amphitheatre, which provides spectator seating for tank and military vehicle demonstrations, takes the form of a grassy hillside leaning against the north wall of the museum. The north-west corner steps down to an outdoor café patio, helping to blur the distinction between outside and inside spaces. It is anticipated that, over time, outdoor exhibits will further animate this area. The dramatic berms that shape the landscape just beyond the library at the west end commemorate Beaumont Hamel, which was transformed by war into a moonscape of bomb craters.

STREET LEVEL

At street level, the building's exterior responds to the site's dual personality: an urban venue in a natural setting. The eastern edge of the building, with its wide views of the Parliamentary Precinct and Wellington Street, expresses the urban, while the western edge works to blend the building into the green riverscape. At the southeast corner, glazed walls offer inviting views into the museum, tempting the curiosity of passersby with a promise of the experience that waits within.

The design was inspired by the unselfish bravery of ordinary Canadian soldiers, as expressed in countless stories and depicted in a number of paintings, such as *Over the Top, Neuville-Vitasse* by Alfred Bastien, in the CWM collection (and shown above).

The building is designed around a complex system of tilting planes that collide and intersect with one another, some at dramatic angles, others with almost imperceptible subtlety. Many of these planes pierce the building envelope, jutting from the outside to the inside. These transitions are most evident at the various skylights, where visitors can see concrete surfaces entering and leaving the museum. These sloping and colliding planes express the tension and upheaval of war, and are a physical representation of the devastation of the land. A gradual process of regeneration is implied in the way the jagged planes come together within the museum to form spaces of memory, contemplation and spirituality.

LA TRAVERSE: A WALK OVER THE MUSEUM

The grass roof and low profile not only integrate the new building into the site, they also connect and mediate spaces within both its macro and micro contexts. On the grand scale, the building links the cityscape with the waterfront, connecting a previously isolated industrial site to its two neighbouring environments, natural and urban. At the scale of the site, the building connects the Common to the south with the Riverside Promenade to the north. To that end it is designed to function as an earth bridge or "little mountain." Visitors can even walk right over the top of the building along a heavily textured pathway.

The roof is accessible to all, including wheelchair users. A gently sloping ramp with a high-friction surface begins on the building's south side, just east of the entrance, and climbs slowly up to the roof. The descent to the north follows a zigzag path down to the Riverside Promenade.

On the walk up from the south, the visitor crosses above the museum's vestibule and passes a long, slender, wedge-shaped window with views into the Foyer below and beyond. Turning a sharp corner to the north, the visitor then enters a concrete trench. The planned future installation of barbed wire fencing just a few metres to the east on the grass roof will intensify the trench experience.

SALUTING THE PEACE TOWER

At the peak of La Traverse the visitor can experience some of the museum's many layers of meaning. To the north, the view is bounded by the copper facade and roof of Regeneration Hall; the upper and southern edges of the frame are created by the inverted L-shaped salute of the Hall of Remembrance. Turning to face east, the visitor will enjoy a moment where the museum's architecture frames a stunning view of the Parliament Buildings in the distance. The museum's roof rises gently to the east, creating a visual plinth for our nation's legislature. Here, at this precise place on La Traverse, the architecture pays silent homage to the Peace Tower, the symbolic home of all Canadians.

MAST OF REMEMBRANCE

La Traverse was meant to be crowned by the "Mast of Remembrance." Almost invisibly, the mast would have pierced the roof of the Hall of Remembrance and then soared heavenward. Trailing from it would have been eleven stainless pierced bars, angled at precisely 90 degrees to the 26.23-degree angle of the sun's rays at 11:00 a.m. on Remembrance Day. This would have been subtle, yet the subtlety would have grown in strength and meaning with each passing year. The mast would have shimmered in the sunlight, unforgettable in the crimson rays of sunset and the silver glint of moonlight. On windy days, it would have hummed mysteriously like a low-pitched harp. The Mast of Remembrance was to be a profound, unpretentious symbol of sacrifice located exactly at the spot where the museum aligns with the Peace Tower and the solar line at 11:00 a.m. on Remembrance Day.

Every project has its ups and its downs, however, and the war museum was no exception. Sadly, the fate of the Mast of Remembrance was a down. Clients and architects need not always agree, but they generally keep each other informed about important decisions such as deleting a budget item that happens to be a Mast of Remembrance. Suffice it to say that, in my view, losing this significant design element without notice was an error, and its absence is a source of sadness for me.

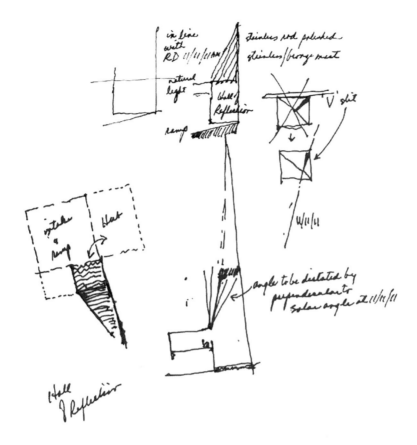

My sadness was aggravated by another decision imposed on the team behind my back: to install a floor tile in the Foyer and other public areas to improve the "look." The floor was to have been finished in grey motley concrete patterned to point in the direction of the Peace Tower; large, black, elongated triangular concrete patterns at strategic locations would have intensified the sense of compression one experiences on entering the Foyer. The decision to add floor tiles added a cost far exceeding the projected cost of the Mast of Remembrance. Of equal or greater significance, it also had a seriously negative impact on the symbolic and visual strength of the Foyer and other public areas, and made it difficult to install heavy artifacts such as tanks or artillery there in the future. The desire to improve the appearance may have been sincere, but in my view the decision was made without an appreciation for our overall vision or the unity of design and usage.

MEMORIAL GARDEN

Also part of the journey over La Traverse lies the unfinished Memorial Garden, patiently waiting for donors. This sunken roof will become a garden to honour Canada's most important events. One idea being contemplated is to display twenty-one free-standing bronze columns or obelisks (representing the twenty-one gun salute), each inscribed with names, images or other references to events important to Canadians in times of peace and war. The garden will be open to the public day and night, summer and winter, and should contribute yet another layer of meaning and tribute.

The visitor will step down into the sunken garden to interact with these bronze "trees"; he or she will be free to touch their surfaces, read the inscriptions and recall the valour and significance of past events. Small hidden searchlights on the top of each column, invisible during the day, will send twenty-one columns of light up into the night sky. In Ottawa, where darkness comes early in winter, drivers on LeBreton Boulevard and across the Ottawa River in Hull will see another perspective of the museum.

Turning west, the view of sunsets year round is remarkable.

CWM AS A CATALYST FOR FUTURE DEVELOPMENTS

The Canadian War Museum is designed to serve as a catalyst for balanced future development of LeBreton Flats and the area beyond. LeBreton Flats is becoming a wonderfully active setting. The NCC is continuing the development of a promenade for walking, jogging, rollerblading and cycling, with connections to the Trans Canada Trail. Immediately to the south of the CWM a new Common, also developed by the NCC, provides open space and parkland for recreation, community festivals and civic celebrations. Despite certain challenges in managing building security and the internal environment of the museum, it seemed wise to build a connection with these flanking amenities into the project design.

To the north across the bridge are Albert and Amelia islands, the dramatic Chaudières Falls and the Domtar industrial site, which has the potential to evolve into a wonderfully integrated gathering place akin to Vancouver's Granville Island. To the south of the Common, the potential exists for a thoughtful, innovative model community combining housing and commerce.

In my view, the creation of an outstanding built environment in this area as a western gateway to Ottawa's Parliamentary Precinct and downtown core is critical to the successful realization of the forty-year dream of developing LeBreton Flats. Nothing short of an integrated, architecturally enlightened model community should be acceptable for Ottawa, the nation's capital.

CONNECTING THROUGH THE MUSEUM

The National Capital Commission requested that no single entrance, either at the front or the back of the building, be given obvious prominence. We took this a step further by creating a museum building with no real front or back. The north entrance facing the river and the Riverside Promenade is the same size and significance as the one looking south towards the Common. The entrances are connected through the generous Foyer.

The public can travel from the riverside to the Common by traversing the roof or through the museum's interior passageway. In this way, the building is not an obstacle on the site, but rather a nexus; it does not divide the site, but connects it together. I hope this design philosophy of connections and linkages will inform and inspire the future development of Albert and Amelia islands and the Domtar industrial site so that, eventually, the dramatic beauty of Chaudières Falls will be woven into an integrated continuum of experiences in and around the museum.

INTERIOR

WHILE THE EXTERIOR PLANES of the building reflect the trauma of war as visited upon the land, the raw materials and tensions of the interior planes express the intensity of an urban streetscape torn and brutalized by battle.

Walls emerge sharp and unrefined from the floors at jagged angles. Concrete is left raw and exposed. Joints of forms are rough. The concrete surfaces were modelled in three patterns: the memorial pattern, used on the exterior and interior of the Hall of Remembrance; the random plywood pattern, which resembles unevenly patched walls and buildings; and the vertical board pattern, which graces most exterior facades and interior walls. The contractors, the Bellai Brothers, were specifically requested to aim for a controlled imperfection, including creating loose joints so that concrete would ooze out from the seams. They achieved magnificent results.

The dramatic angled walls rise from interior floors that are also canted, skewing one's sense of equilibrium. The aim is to provoke a sense of unease within visitors sufficient to release some of their physical and emotional inhibitions. We wanted the architecture and materials to jar people into a fresh consciousness, to heighten their awareness, not only of place but also of themselves.

THE POWER OF ABSENCE

Many of the museum's walls and spaces are intentionally austere and free of distractions. Emptiness and silence have a profound strength; they give the visitor room to release personal thoughts, memories and emotions, so that everyone will fill the space in his or her own unique way. In their rush to entertain and stimulate, museums are too often cluttered with inappropriate posters and paraphernalia, leaving few or no places for silence and emptiness. This is not the case with the new Canadian War Museum, where the power of absence is given special honour.

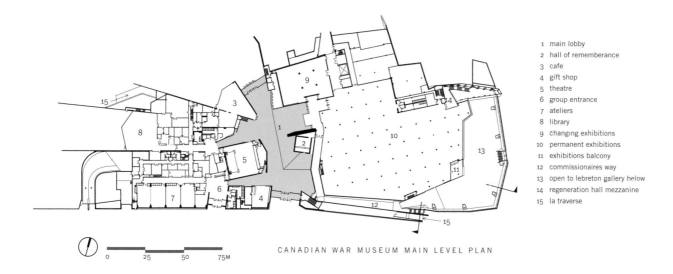

1 main lobby
2 hall of rememberance
3 cafe
4 gift shop
5 theatre
6 group entrance
7 ateliers
8 library
9 changing exhibitions
10 permanent exhibitions
11 exhibitions balcony
12 commissionaires way
13 open to lebreton gallery below
14 regeneration hall mezzanine
15 la traverse

0   25   50   75M

CANADIAN WAR MUSEUM MAIN LEVEL PLAN

GENERAL ORGANIZATION

FREE ZONE

The Foyer divides the museum into two parts. The area to the west is a "free" zone independent of the exhibition areas. Without having to pay admission, the public can enjoy the waterfront café with its outdoor terrace and wonderful views; browse in the boutique; partake in workshops in the four ateliers; visit and make use of the military history research centre manned by caring staff and knowledgeable volunteers; and attend events such as lectures, audiovisual exhibitions, dramatic and musical plays, and banquets in the 250-seat Barney Danson Theatre. Administrative offices, curatorial laboratories and elevators to the two levels of underground parking are also located west of the Foyer. These "free" areas can be operated independently without opening the whole museum.

PAYING ZONE

All areas requiring admission are to the east of the Foyer and all are manned by friendly tour guides, volunteers and veterans. These include the Temporary Gallery, the Art Gallery, the Permanent Gallery, Regeneration Hall, the LeBreton Gallery (the large military artifact area) and the Commissionaire's Way. From the Foyer and ticket-purchasing counter, a gentle ramp leads eastwards up to the Permanent Gallery. The visitor can then proceed to the Art Gallery, Temporary Gallery, Regeneration

Hall, LeBreton Gallery and Commissionaire's Way or to the Balcony located above the LeBreton Gallery. The Balcony is an ideal spot from which to gaze over the expanse of space below and to drink in fabulous views of the city and the Parliamentary Precinct beyond the expansive glazing that defines the building's southeast edge.

ALIGNMENTS

As well as the clear connection through the Foyer in the north-south direction, there is a more subtle alignment running east-west. The Barney Danson Theatre, Regeneration Hall and the entrance to the galleries all align with and focus on the Peace Tower; these links are explained in further detail below.

FOYER

"Like going to the depths of hell to resurrect the soul." These words, spoken to me by a woman consulted early in the project, echoed in my head. So did the solemn music of Wagner and fractured images of the beautiful ugliness of contemporary dance. From this imagined choreography of words, music and movement emerged my inspiration for the Foyer.

The Foyer provokes in all who enter it a sense of compression, a fear that the ceiling is pressing down upon them as they adjust to the sloping floor beneath their feet. This initial feeling of confinement gives way to a sense of release as the eye travels upwards to the rhythmically undulating ceiling and the junctions with the walls, where natural light enters from a series of long, narrow skylights. The vast space gradually takes form as the shifting light flickers across it. Sunlight and moonlight play in turn upon the simple palette of concrete and recycled copper, giving apparent life and animation to otherwise inert material. Light creating shadow, revealing form and expressing space is as much a part of the architecture here as steel and concrete.

Nestled within the Foyer like a building within a building is an austere, nine-by-nine-metre cube: the Hall of Remembrance. The cube is oriented on an independent axis that seems at odds with the rest of the building. To emphasize its independence and importance, the Hall of Remembrance is surrounded by dramatic natural sun- and moonlight. This natural light beckons the visitor to enter deeper into the Foyer and counters the initial sense of foreboding with a sense of quiet spiritual uplift, encouraging further explorations.

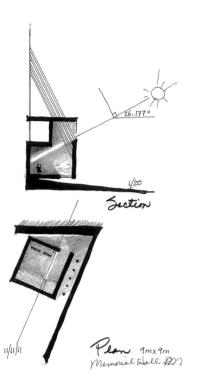

HALL OF REMEMBRANCE

A place of quiet reflection, the Hall of Remembrance honours the memories of veterans and the heroic lives sacrificed for Canada and for the ideals of peace and democracy. At first glance, it does not seem to fit with its immediate surrounding in shape, location or orientation. It is positioned on the exact spot where, on November 11 at 11:00 a.m., the path of the sun intersects with the view corridor to the Peace Tower.

From the Foyer, a narrow ramp, secretive and almost hidden, ascends to a triangular Antechamber, then turns nearly 360 degrees to lead the visitor into the Hall of Remembrance. The ramp begins as an elongated, triangular tunnel, narrow and sloping upwards to heighten the visitor's disorientation with an added sense of claustrophobia. Again, light mediates the experience, offering the reassurance of the familiar: spotlights in the floor create lighting effects in the narrow access that are animated by the passing of each visitor.

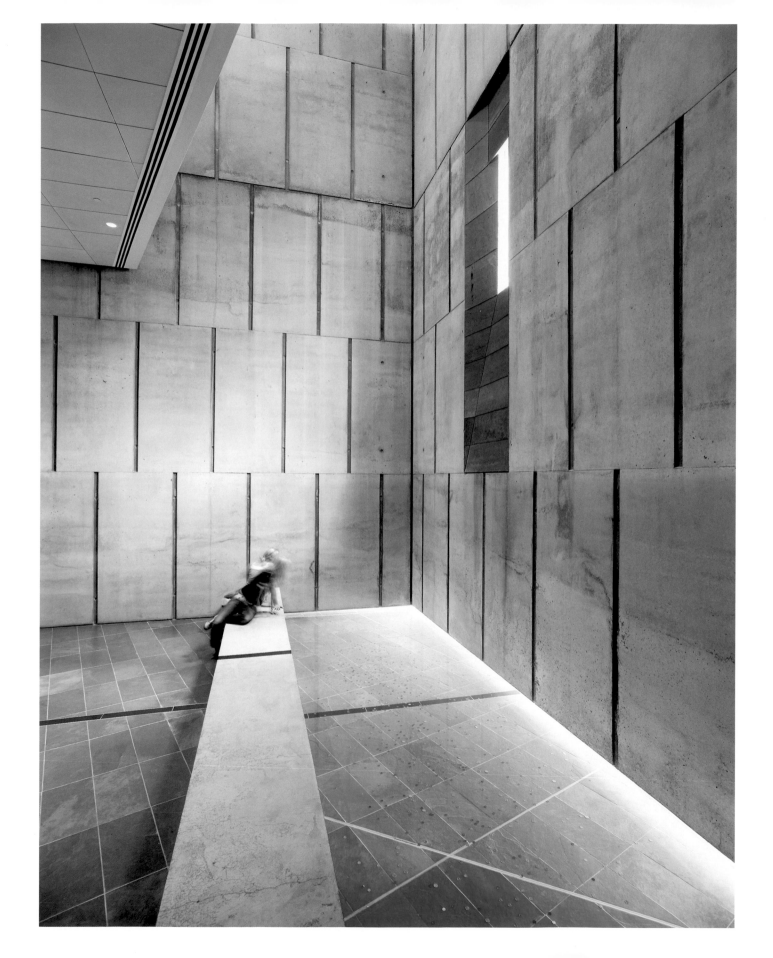

Disorientation yields to serenity as the visitor emerges into the Hall of Remembrance itself. The "Last Post" played softly on a bugle on Remembrance Day filtering into this space is inspirational. The hall is sombre and austere, yet calm and meditative. Here, the power of light is not to be glorified. Daylight is suppressed, controlled and filtered. A sliver of a wedge-shaped clerestory window lets in the subtle glow of sunsets. Light is also filtered into the chamber through a shallow reflecting pool contained on three sides by a slender horizontal corner window at the base of the south, east and west walls. This window is as high as the pool is deep. From the Foyer, visitors see it as translucent green-blue water moving against the smooth grey concrete facade of the cube and seeming to float over it.

Inside the cubic chamber, simple geometry is respected: horizontal and vertical planes meet at perfect right angles and there are no sloping canted surfaces to distort the equilibrium. The desired psychological effect is one of strength, balance and inner peace in total respect for those who made sacrifices to preserve our Canadian way of life.

The reflective pool soothes the senses with the promise of the regenerative qualities of water. From a hidden source in the clerestory, a single drop of water is released every twenty seconds—one cycle of calm breathing in meditation—into the calm pool, creating quiet ripples and drawing out thoughts and memories. In the evening, the pool is illuminated, casting a glow that spreads through the water and the glazed pool walls and onto the sloped floor outside in the Foyer.

THE POWER OF THE SUN

Each year at 11:00 a.m. on Remembrance Day, a shaft of sunlight will penetrate the Hall of Remembrance and shine upon the original headstone of the Unknown Soldier. For this powerful moment, we have choreographed the union of space, time, nature and architecture. At the eleventh hour of the eleventh day of the eleventh month, a ray of sunlight intersects the sightline to the Peace Tower and penetrates the museum to illuminate the headstone, mounted 173 centimetres (five feet eight inches) above the

floor to represent the average height of the Canadian soldiers who fought in the two world wars. The precise trajectory of the sun at this moment is recorded in a black line that transects the entire museum. From its centre within the Hall of Remembrance, this black sun trail crosses the floor before heading north through the Antechamber into the Permanent Gallery and south through the Foyer and Vestibule to the exterior sidewalk and through the Common to LeBreton Boulevard. Moreover, a white light cove set into the ceiling of the Foyer runs parallel to the black line on the floor and leads the eye to the Hall of Remembrance. It is hard to imagine a better way to immortalize our Remembrance Day in Ottawa.

THE ANTECHAMBER

One wall of the triangular Antechamber is clad with patinated copper recycled from the Library of Parliament. To acknowledge its genesis, the wall is oriented to align with the Peace Tower. The use of fifty-year-old copper not only strengthens the museum's connections with our parliament and past but also treats the viewer to a unique architectural element of such beauty that some have called it art. The natural light that enters through a narrow slit between this wall and the concrete wall of the Hall of Remembrance further enhances the experience. The viewer can decide if this is art or architecture; either way, there is great satisfaction in knowing that, among the many artifacts newly housed in the museum, these lovingly hand-worked copper panels from our parliament buildings will be preserved forever.

And there is yet another dimension to the significance of these carefully preserved copper panels, a human dimension revealed in the moving story of one tradesman. Working to install the recycled copper, this young man discovered his uncle's signature from about five decades ago on the back of one panel. The uncle, still in good health, was invited to the site to celebrate his nephew's work and the discovery of his personal mark. To continue or perhaps begin a tradition, the young man then signed his own name to the back of a new copper panel with the hope that, in another fifty years, a future relation might discover it in a similar way. This new panel bearing the young man's signature is now part of the exterior roofing of the new museum—only time will tell if history repeats itself. I was personally moved by this wonderful story of human connection through work and art—in many ways, what this new museum is all about.

THE SLIT OF LIGHT

The narrow slit at the westerly apex of the Antechamber separates the copper wall and the concrete wall of the Hall of Remembrance. From inside the Antechamber, visitors see the sunlight and the shadows from a skylight. As the light spills through the opening and falls on the diagonal pattern of the patinated copper wall, it forms what my colleague Alex Rankin calls "Jacob's Ladder." I hope the slit of light will evoke a sense of unity and universal reverence in visitors before they make a sharp turn to the left and enter the Hall of Remembrance.

THE GALLERIES

Although we were commissioned to design the museum building, we were excluded from any involvement in exhibit design right from the outset. Since neither the concept nor the design of the future exhibits had been clearly defined when we began the architectural process, we designed all the gallery areas on a nine-metre grid as flexible, neutral, serviced spaces with generous ceilings of varied heights. This approach gives curators, museum staff and exhibit designers a set of tools and a free hand to shape walls, raise floors, lower ceilings, hang objects, create spaces and vary colours and lighting as they wish. The galleries are designed as "Tool Boxes for Change"—unencumbered, adaptable spaces that can accommodate future needs and facilitate ongoing innovation.

I feel grateful that our proposal for expanding the Permanent Gallery, based on our past museum experience, was eventually heeded. As a result, the gallery space was increased by more than 50 per cent.

PUBLIC WASHROOMS

Details such as public washrooms may seem uninspiring, but it is an error to underestimate the importance of their design. I was reminded of this fact during our public input sessions, when several veterans asked me not to spend any money embellishing the washrooms. One veteran thought "wartime primitive" would be sufficient. We explored the possibility of recreating such a look, including features like the then-typical metal trough urinals and communal wash basins. Not surprisingly, we found that, while it would have been fun and wonderfully nostalgic, it was too expensive.

So, to my veteran readers, I would like to acknowledge that your sage counsel was borne in mind when we designed the washrooms, our key design concept being "economy." The WCs are simple rooms, painted and tiled in one colour—a World War II hospital green, the very colour that haunted my brethren architects in the 1940s, '50s and '60s. The colour originally selected was a pure clear red. Although many, myself included, would have loved to use such a dramatic and effective colour for its contrast with the rest of the museum, others ultimately rejected it as "unsafe" and "too disturbing." So now the hospital-green walls, ceilings and floors await wartime posters, maps and bulletins.

LEBRETON GALLERY, LARGE ARTIFACT DISPLAY AREA

With its dramatic expanse of exterior glazing articulating the southeast corner of the building, the LeBreton Gallery is a lens into the museum. Here, where vehicle traffic is heaviest, the gallery is an architectural "billboard" that announces the Canadian War Museum to passersby and the city. From the inside looking out, visitors are rewarded with magnificent skyline views of downtown Ottawa and the Parliamentary Precinct.

The LeBreton Gallery houses the museum's collection of large and heavy artifacts of war, including tanks, trucks, artillery and planes. The exterior glazing is inclined outwards and patterned with a mix of frosted, clear and solid panels, which brings the surface to life; these panels will eventually be used for audiovisual presentations on

either side, heightening the experience of visitors both inside and outside the museum. The towering demising wall at the mezzanine level is also inclined and can be animated with colourful images, patterns and movies to engage patrons and passersby. The visual impact of this wall is noticeable from outside the museum and is particularly effective in darkened conditions, be they winter afternoons or warm summer evenings.

Acoustically, the space was designed to be slightly hard and bouncy, to welcome the swing music of World War II. Music—notably the big-band sounds of such greats as Glenn Miller, Artie Shaw, Woody Herman, Duke Ellington and Tommy Dorsey and the classic jazz and blues of legends like Bunk Johnson, Albert Nicholas, Kid Ory and Coleman Hawkins—was an important inspiration. Such sounds wonderfully enhance the sense of time and place within the LeBreton Gallery, with its numerous large tanks and other artifacts from World Wars I and II. In my mind, this is an amazing venue for lively and nostalgic parties, with an orchestra, jazz group or swing band playing right on the floor next to the large artifacts or from the Balcony overlooking the gallery. I am eagerly awaiting my invitation to such a happy, jumping event!

THE COMMISSIONAIRE'S WAY: A SLOPING CORRIDOR

Parallel to the ascending ramp of La Traverse but running along the interior of the
south building facade lies the Commissionaire's Way, a major public ramp. This sloping
corridor runs up from the LeBreton Gallery to connect with the Foyer, bringing the
visitor full circle. It is one of the museum's non-programmed spaces, a broad corridor
detailed and dramatized to enhance the war museum experience. The flanking walls to
the north and south slope steeply upwards in parallel but opposing directions. Along the
Way is a generous open slope that visitors can lounge upon, semi-prone.

The corridor is lit from two sources: natural light entering through a series of small
apertures along the south wall and artificial light emanating from a row of tank lights
mounted on the same wall. The tank lights with their red halos heighten the visitors'
sense of excitement and disorientation as they navigate this raw concrete passageway.

MORSE CODE MESSAGES

The windows in the Commissionaire's Way are more than just a series of small apertures. The sun spots they create spell out a message in Morse code: CWM and MCG, the initials for Canadian War Museum / Musée canadien de la guerre in both official languages. More than just a cryptic system of communication, this was an innovative way to create a pattern of fenestration, which we used again in the small high windows of Regeneration Hall. Looking up at the copper facade of the hall's sloping tower, the visitor can read "Lest we forget" in both official languages. Only in a war museum could Morse code find a home as both a unique signage system and an innovative lighting technique.

REGENERATION HALL

Regeneration Hall is a repository of experiences that speak to the future and to hope. Spiritual without being religious, Regeneration Hall is a place of rest and thought, sublime and subdued, solemn and quiet, dramatic and memorable. This is the place in the museum where an unglamorous, necessary back stairwell becomes an architectural exhibit in and of itself. To accomplish this without raising the overall budget was a challenge.

Most visitors enter the diagonally sloping vertical space of Regeneration Hall at mezzanine level. Subdued lighting slows the pace, forcing them to pause as their eyes adjust. The sound of the wind, recorded in the same space during construction, can be heard, softly at first and then more clearly. Some visitors may find this sound to be strange and unsettling; others will be moved by it, and many will not hear it all.

Regeneration
Hall
R Moriyama

A brief elaboration may be appropriate here. During one of my construction reviews on site, Alex Rankin and I were chatting and he mentioned the way the wind whistled and sometimes gently howled through the enclosed but unfinished hall. I rushed over and, sure enough, the wind was humming through the perforations of the wall cladding. Although it was a little more metallic, the sound was very similar to the one I remember hearing in the tree house, eerie yet comforting. I was excited—it was as if my first sound-inspired sketch had come to life. By God's will, Joe Geurts, the museum's director and CEO, was on the site conducting a tour. Forgetting my manners I jumped in, interrupted the group, and asked Joe if he could get someone to record the sound for use in an exhibit. He did, and, as the saying goes, the rest is history.

Back on the landing, visitors look up and take in the space of Regeneration Hall. Long, narrow and dramatically high, this is an enormous, slender wedge that may seem like a giant fin or a sloping tower. The exposed steel structure and walls appear wobbly and imperfect.

Straight ahead, in the thin edge of the vertical wedge, a slender, triangular window soars from the floor to the very top of the space. At the spot where a single pane of glass interrupts the mezzanine guardrail, visitors catch a tightly framed view of the Peace Tower silhouetted against the sky.

A staircase fabricated of sheet steel leads down from the mezzanine to the main floor. Shifting sun spots spelling out "Lest we forget" and "N'oublions jamais" in Morse code move across the slanting north wall of the exposed steel structure, which has been made to seem uneven and unnerving. Especially on sunny days, the ever-changing dappled light reminds us of the ephemeral nature of human life.

As the visitor descends the stairs, the perspective shifts. The view of the Peace Tower is lost, just as peace itself can be so easily lost. In its place a compelling sculpture—the original plaster maquette of Walter Alward's *Hope*—soars into view. It seems to float in front of the window, whose translucent glazing creates a soft backdrop and muffles the busy urban view and noise outside. The visitor is drawn down to the main level and on

towards the dramatically lit figure. There is a sense of ascension, but this is an optical illusion; the floor is actually flat. The intent here is to impose an experience upon the visitor as he or she moves through the main floor. While the thoughts and emotional responses of each person will differ, it is my hope that Regeneration Hall will provoke unease for the future and a compensating sense of humanity and hope.

I am sure not many structural engineers are asked to "design a totally exposed steel structural—naked, uncovered and wobbly—to express a feeling of hope amongst unease and instability." This is what we demanded of Michael Allen and the staff of Adjeleian Allen Rubeli in creating the structure of Regeneration Hall. Working closely together with our joint venture and Walters Inc., supplier and erector of steel structure, they did a remarkable job, forging a series of double-hinged arches, each one different from the next. These steel sections were so well designed that, on delivery to the site, they snapped together without a hitch. The structure, even the space, feels wobbly—as we used to say during World War II, "Jumping Jiminy! Perfect!"

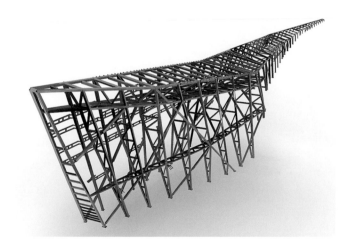

CONSTRUCTION

"I'M AN EIGHTY-SIX-YEAR-OLD VETERAN. *When are you going to finish this darned war museum?*

I want to see it before I see Him!"

These are oddly compelling words for an architect, more compelling, I must admit, than any timeline established by the client. I received a great deal of advice from the veterans we consulted: "Don't glorify war!" "Make us proud!" "Don't spend too much money, but do a great job!" In the end, I wanted to achieve a building that would respect all of the genuine views we had heard.

There were a few key milestones along the way.

SOD-TURNING   The sod-turning ceremony took place on November 5, 2002, less than a year after the design process had begun and a mere four months after our final design had been approved. By then, the NCC had arranged for the removal of every inch of contaminated soil on the site, right down to the bedrock. It is amusing to recall that several cubic metres of clean soil had to be brought in and carefully placed onto the bedrock, just so that the dignitaries had some actual soil to turn!

At a meeting with the client and other consultants on November 15, 2001, I predicted that as officially programmed, the war museum building would cost $225 CAD per square foot. The cost I predicted was significantly less than the cost per square foot for other national institutional buildings in Ottawa, namely $350 CAD per square foot for the National Gallery and something in the range of $325 to $350 CAD for the Museum of Civilization.* It was also much lower than figures from $300 to $500 USD per square foot considered acceptable in international circles. The capital cost at completion in 2005 was $218 CAD per square foot, seven dollars less than predicted.

I cannot pretend that meeting such a low budget was easy. My biggest heroes on the project, the real champions, are the joint-venture members. They battled uphill the entire time, enduring relentless needling and haggling, not over important ideas or concepts but over micromanagement of every detail. I will not elaborate on the short-sighted bureaucratic culture that we struggled against every day. Suffice it to say that in the end, our faith in the importance of the project to Canadians and our resolve to get things right won through.

Departing from the war museum for a moment, but still on the subject of management, cost, quality and timing control, Moriyama & Teshima Architects had recently worked on another larger-scale project of equal domestic and international importance: the National Museum of Saudi Arabia and the King Abdul Aziz Historical Centre (see photo, page 119, bottom). This complex, won by our firm in an international design competition, was built to launch the celebrations of Saudi Arabia's hundred-year anniversary. It was completed in thirty months using fifteen tall cranes and, at times, over four thousand workers on a 34-hectare (83-acre) site in central Riyadh, the capital. It was finished on time and under budget, proving that with good organization, focused priorities, genuine teamwork and great leadership, such extremely forced scheduling difficulties can be overcome without sacrificing quality or dissipating human energy.

* Updated to the 2003 Canadian dollar.

Fresh from this experience, we decided to employ a construction consultant system on the CWM project to gain time and still control quality and cost. This management technique was similar to the one we had used during the construction of the Ottawa-Carleton Regional Headquarters, now Ottawa's City Hall—a project that was completed under budget. The Bata Shoe Museum (above) in Toronto was completed 10 per cent under budget, and some of the savings were used to commission an extensive stained-glass artwork.

We also completed the $200-million CAD Canadian embassy in Tokyo (opposite, top) ahead of schedule and at no cost to the Canadian taxpayers. Once again we proved that, with enlightened leadership and teamwork, wonderful quality design could be realized. The intriguing specifics of this achievement, however, are a story for another day.

FROM TREE HOUSE TO WAR MUSEUM

IT IS DIFFICULT TO EXPRESS how privileged I feel at being chosen to design and oversee the building of Canada's new war museum. I am grateful to have had the support of all the talented and dedicated individuals in the MTA-GRC team. It was truly a joint venture made in heaven. The experience was exhilarating, challenging and profoundly spiritual.

I am not afraid to talk about this project as my legacy to the people of this country I love because I am not afraid to express the pride I feel when I reflect upon all we have accomplished. It is my hope that in this institution, in the architecture and all that it evokes, people will find solace, compassion, understanding and inspiration. More importantly, I hope that each person will experience something unique—a personal awakening like the one I experienced in my modest tree house way back when.

In the design of the museum, the architectural team and I have tried to balance nature and urbanity, good design and economy, reality and imagination, war and hope, darkness and light, sustainability and functionality, all to bring clarity to the varied voices of Canadians without destroying the ambiguity of plurality. The result is a tribute to all veterans and to those who sacrificed their lives to preserve our way of life. It is a tribute to those who, through unselfish deed and truth of spirit, provide us with the backbone of inspiration, for life or architecture or both. It is a tribute to all those who worked so hard and gave so much of themselves to design and build this special place. And finally, it is a tribute to those team members who understood the bigger vision and who fought tenaciously and religiously for it. Thank you.

In this country, and just a boy, my love and faith were tested; but also in this country, as a son, a father, a husband and an architect, my love and faith have been nurtured and—ultimately—liberated.

In the architecture of the Canadian War Museum I have tried to celebrate Canada, the land I love, and tried to honour the ordinary people who went to war and became extraordinary.

In the memorial tradition, I would like to close this document with a dedication:

To all Canadians and citizens worldwide who suffered injustice, discrimination and deprivation, yet transcended with humanity, creativity, compassion and thoughtful action to enrich all of our lives;

To my wife, Sachi—my life-partner, my best friend and a dedicated mother—for her love of architecture, generosity, tolerance, understanding and gentle encouragement to "go for it";

To my children—Michi, Murina, Midori, Jason and Ajon—a father's everlasting thanks for enriching and enhancing my life; my prayer for their health, happiness and long life with their spouses, their children and their children's children;

To my mother, Elsie Nobuko, for sharing with me her love of the arts and for teaching me to work hard and "to give more than you receive"; and

To my father, John Michi, a son's love and eternal gratitude for giving my life meaning, and for the powerful gift of a simple poem that propelled and sustained me:

> *Into God's temple of eternity,*
> *Drive a nail of gold.*

PICTURE CREDITS

GRC = Griffiths Rankin Cook Architects
MTA = Moriyama & Teshima Architects
CWM = Canadian War Museum
CMC = Canadian Museum of Civilization

Page ii, ramp into the Hall of Remembrance showing the floor lights that mark the entrance, © Tom Arban

Page x, detailed view inside the Hall of Remembrance, © Emmanuelle van Rutten, GRC

Page 3, sketch of childhood tree house, © Raymond Moriyama

Pages 4–5 and 8–9, the Commissionaire's Way under construction, © Harry Foster, CMC

Page 7, concrete workers placing rebar (reinforcing bars) in one of the walls of Commissionaire's Way, © Emmanuelle van Rutten, GRC

Page 9 top, view of steel bracing one of the theatre walls during construction, © Michael Conway, GRC

Page 9 bottom, south side of the building under construction, © Brian Rudy, MTA

Page 10, angled wall and protruding rebar, © Emmanuelle van Rutten, GRC

Page 11, Nathalie Marion walking under a leaning concrete wall, © Peter Rankin, GRC

Page 12, Silhouette of person and scaffolding during construction, © Michael Conway, GRC

Page 14, the client and design team in the MTA boardroom, © MTA/GRC

Page 15 top left, Gene Ascenzi, Diarmuid Nash, Brian Rudy, Greg Karavelis and Nathalie Marion at Vimy House, © MTA/GRC

Page 15 top right, Raymond Moriyama and Alexander Rankin, © Michael Conway, GRC

Page 15 bottom, most of the MTA/GRC team, © Michael Conway, GRC

Page 19, Diarmuid Nash, Raymond Moriyama and Alexander Rankin by Hall of Remembrance, © Michael Conway, GRC

Pages 20–21 and 27, aerial view of Passchendaele village on June 16, 1917, George Metcalf Archival Collection, CWM 20020111-001

Page 23 left, urban destruction in Caen, Normandy, July 1944, National Archives of Canada, PA-116510

Page 23 right, trench warfare

Page 24, women working in a munitions factory, National Archives of Canada, C-18734

Page 26 top and bottom, Passchendaele village after the battle, 1917

Page 28 left, autumn leaves, © Malak 1995

Page 28 right, Lake Huron, © Joseph Hanus 2002

Page 29 top, Qu'Appelle Valley, Saskatchewan, © Malak 1995

Page 29 bottom, Ottawa river near Pembroke, Ontario, © Malak 1995

Page 30, *The Stretcher-Bearer Party* by Cyril Barraud (1877–1965), 1918, © CWM [AN 19710261-0019] Beaverbrook Collection of War Art

Page 31 left, *The Defenders: Breaking the Sword*, plaster maquette for the Vimy Memorial by Walter Allward (1875–1955) 1920s, © CMC

Page 31 right top & bottom, the CWM collection, © Spacesaver Corporation, photos by Image Images Photography

Page 32, *Parachute Riggers* by Paraskeva Clark (1898–1986), © CWM [AN 19710261-5679] Beaverbrook Collection of War Art

Page 33 left, *War in the Air* by C.R.W. Nevinson (1889–1946), 1918, © CWM [AN 19710261-0517] Beaverbrook Collection of War Art

Page 33 right, *Via Dolorosa, Ortona* by Charles Comfort (1900–1994), date unknown, © CWM [AN 12402] Beaverbrook Collection of War Art

Page 34 top, museum site from bridge upriver, © Brian Rudy, MTA

Page 34 middle, aerial view of LeBreton Flats, © National Capital Commission

Page 34 bottom, grasses on the site, © Drew Wensley, MTA

Page 37 bottom, *Infantry, near Nijmegen, Holland* by Alexander Colville (1920–), 1946, © CWM [AN 19710261-2079] Beaverbrook Collection of War Art

Page 39, conceptual sketch of the wind, © Raymond Moriyama

Pages 40–41, 12 of the 64 schematic sketch models, © MTA/GRC

Page 42, renderings of three conceptual designs, © Cicada Design, MTA/GRC

Page 43, rendering of the final design, © Dan Henhoeffer, MTA/GRC

Pages 44–45, reclaimed copper wall, © Tom Arban

Page 46 left, Australian troops at third Battle of Ypres, 1917, Australian War Memorial, IWM PC0029 Neg. No. E(Aus) 1220

Page 46 right, Mountie at Beaumont Hamel

Page 47, rendering of the final design, © Peter Roper, MTA/GRC

Page 48, conceptual sketches of two major building axes: 11/11 and the Peace Tower, © Raymond Moriyama

Page 49, drawing showing view corridor to Peace Tower and Parliament, © MTA/GRC

Pages 50–51 and 60, La Traverse, © Tom Arban

Page 52 top, site plan, © Williams, Asselin, Ackaoui et associés Inc.

Page 52 bottom, aerial view from the northwest, © Canadian Aerial Photo Corporation

Page 53, concrete wall and grass berms at west end of Vimy Street, © Tom Arban

Page 55 top, 100-level plan, © MTA/GRC

Page 55 bottom, 300-level plan, © MTA/GRC

Page 56, sloped concrete wall at the junction between LeBreton Gallery and La Traverse, © Tom Arban

Page 57, *Over the Top, Neuville-Vitasse* by Alfred Bastien (1873–1955), 1918, © CWM [AN 19710261-0057] Beaverbrook Collection of War Art

Page 58, rendering of the final design, © Peter Roper, MTA/GRC

Pages 58–59, north elevation from across the river, © Tom Arban

ABOUT RAYMOND MORIYAMA

RAYMOND MORIYAMA is one of Canada's most respected architects. Among his award-winning projects are the Japanese Canadian Cultural Centre, the Ontario Science Centre, the Scarborough Civic Centre, the Toronto Reference Library, the Bata Shoe Museum and the Bank of Montreal's Institute for Learning, all in Toronto; the Ottawa-Carleton Regional Headquarters (now Ottawa City Hall); Science North in Sudbury; the Canadian Embassy in Tokyo; the 100 Year Vision, 20 Year Plan and 5 Year Strategy Plan for Niagara Falls; the National Museum of Saudi Arabia in Riyadh, won in an international design competition; and, most recently, the new Canadian War Museum in Ottawa. His firm, Moriyama & Teshima Architects, has received more than one hundred awards.

Born in Vancouver, Raymond Moriyama received his Bachelor of Architecture from the University of Toronto in 1954 and Master of Architecture in Urban Design from McGill University in 1957. Since founding his own firm in 1958 he has received many personal honours including the Royal Architectural Institute of Canada gold medal, the highest national honour bestowed on an individual architect; an honorary fellowship from the American Institute of Architects; ten honorary doctorates; the Confederation of Canada Medal, and the Golden Jubilee Medal. An Officer of the Order of Canada and a Fellow of the Royal Society of Arts (U.K.) and the Royal Architectural Institute of Canada, he has been named on *Maclean's* Honour Roll as a "Canadian Who Made a Difference" and received the Order of Ontario and the Order of the Rising Sun, Gold Rays with Rosette (Japan). In the spring of 2001, he was elected chancellor of Brock University, the first architect in Canada to receive such an honour.

He and his wife, Sachi, have five grown children, three boys and two girls; two are now architects and partners. They are blessed with ten grandchildren, so far.